Dear Substitute Teacher

Margaret Sigel

with Pamela Adler Routh,
Consulting Substitute Teacher

Lost Coast Press

Fort Bragg, California

Dear Substitute Teacher
Copyright © 1997 by Margaret Sigel

For information, phone (707) 964-9520. For bookseller and
library discounts or VISA and MasterCard orders, please call
(800) 883-7782.

Lost Coast Press
155 Cypress Street
Fort Bragg CA 95437

ISBN No. 1-882897-10-2

LCCN No. 96-80310

Cover design by Liz Peterson

Printed in Canada

First Edition

10 9 8 7 6 5 4 3 2 1

Contents

Preface

THE MAJORITY OF URBAN SUBSTITUTE TEACHERS WORK IN isolation, with little steady, supportive contact with other substitute teachers, permanent teachers, school administrators, or district administrators. Substitute teachers in San Francisco were more fortunate; for the decade of 1981 to 1991, the grass roots San Francisco Substitute Teachers Organization (SFSTO) served as an independent substitute teachers union, representing substitutes working in the San Francisco Unified School District. SFSTO brought in two contracts and may have been the only independent substitute teachers union to do so. During the 1980's I attended meetings and met Pamela Adler Routh, among other active substitutes. She was serving as an officer of SFSTO, which she had done since 1982. She was Vice-President of SFSTO and continued to serve as a union officer even after SFSTO joined with the United Educators of San Francisco in 1991. Because we had a means to meet and communicate, Pam and I were able to share ideas and reactions with each other. The result was *Dear Substitute Teacher*.

Dear Fellow Substitute Teachers:

PLEASE FEEL WELCOME TO SHARE THIS ESSAY WITH other teachers, parents, principals, and concerned citizens. However, this essay is directed to you, our colleagues, both beginning and experienced substitute teachers who may have shared some of our difficulties and are looking for a change for the better in the public school system of California. As matters now stand, it is we who are in the best position to make sensible recommendations to bring about that change.

You may ask, "How is this possible?"

I. What is the substitute teachers' place on the educational totem pole?

As I'm sure you know, we are the lowest ranking members on the educational totem pole. Even the clerks, custodians, and cafeteria workers are more highly regarded and sometimes better paid than are we. In fact, the nickname "sub" for substitute teacher indicates very clearly that some administrators and classroom teachers have not realized that this becomes a pejorative term indicating that they may consider us substandard, sub-normal and unqualified teachers. In many schools, the principal and faculty will, without thought or consideration, routinely say things to lower our self-esteem and make our teaching life more difficult. Substitute teachers are denied the benefits and safeguards given to all other employees of the educational system. In order to balance their inadequate budgets, many school districts have purposely hired substitute teachers at low wages, denied the benefits, and refused to negotiate with substitute teachers as a group. There is no rational excuse at the present time for this kind of behavior on the part of school district administrative personnel.

Changes are a necessity. In spite of all the pretty pictures on the bulletin boards and all the "new programs" which are started and publicized each year, the public schools have long been in a state of crisis; student test results and lack of on-the-job proficiency after graduation have been a continuing disgrace, as noted by many news articles and studies. In spite of some positive fluctuations in test results, many teachers realize that despite their best efforts, their classes fall far short of state standards. When we substitute teachers walk into many classes, we see those shortcomings very clearly. It is then an uphill task for the substitute teacher to maintain control of discipline, to try to get through lesson plans, let alone teach new concepts. This dismal state of affairs need never have happened, and it does not need to continue. However, it will continue unless the members of the teaching profession change their thinking and act on that change. So far, that seems unlikely to happen. The substitute teacher, however, in many cases, has touched bottom and has nowhere to go except up. Although you may well understand all this, you may not have considered why we are in the best position to make recommendations, or that we can take some action for change.

II. What do substitute teachers really want? There are five basic tenets.

For the most part, what follows is our sustained argument for changes in tradition, attitude, and a request for understanding of the role of the substitute teacher. Some of the changes which we are requesting in disciplinary tradition may also be helpful to regular classroom teachers, but it is up to those teachers and their unions to use whatever they find applicable and make their own requests to their school boards. We have gone to such lengths to clarify our position since it has been our experience, particularly in Oakland and San Francisco, that resistance to our stated requested changes has been strong and unremitting. Perhaps this resistance has been particularly directed toward substitute teachers alone. Change in the teaching profession has been slower than in almost any other profession. Even permanent teachers have had an uphill battle to get their school boards to listen to their requests for change. By contrast to nearly every other profession, teachers have no control over the economic basis by which they are supported or the conditions under which they are employed. Substitute teachers have even less control than regular teachers in these matters. If you also have found this to be so, you may wish to choose and elaborate your points of argument from those which follow.

Unfortunately, over the years, we have found that reasonable argument is not what the general tax-paying public or public school administrators wish to hear. Nor have they chosen to act upon it. Therefore, in our last section, we have outlined some action which you might try to use if you are committed to working in a worst-case classroom in a worst-case school and district. Even if you feel that you cannot follow our directions step-by-step, you may find that you can adopt some of our basic tenets. These are:

1) That children must learn that their ACTIONS HAVE CONSEQUENCES.

2) That teachers consider disciplinary action as a LEARNING EXPERIENCE FOR THE STUDENT.

3) That the substitute teacher has the right to dismiss disruptive students without fearing prejudice to his evaluation or prejudice against his re-employment in that school or school district.

4) That "in-house" suspension in a supervised area of the school should be promoted as the disciplinary policy of a school district.

5) That substitute teachers should be paid at the same rate and scale and with the same benefits as permanent teachers.

III. Why should substitute teachers be asked to give advice to committees studying the school system?

On December 12 and 13, 1989, State Superintendent of Public Instruction, Bill Honig, held a "Summit Meeting" of educators to confer on the condition of Public Instruction and what could and should be done to improve it in California. He and members of his staff refused to invite any members of the San Francisco Substitute Teachers Organization to represent substitute teachers. This prevented us from conferring and contributing our knowledge and experience. He politely said that he didn't have room for us in the conference center and hoped we would understand. (Pam and I went to the summit and were unceremoniously "kicked out.")

The members of Mr. Honig's committee doubtless had much specialized expertise, but we suspected that few, if any, had the broad spectrum of experience and were able to see the larger picture in the same way as teachers who have had broad and extensive experience as substitute teachers. It is possible that committee members may also have had specific "axes to grind," or were unwilling to boldly speak out on such key issues as student discipline and better ways to manage it. Unless people have had long experience as substitute teachers, or have been in a number of the classrooms recently, they will lose touch with the present generation of students and the problems which substitute teachers must now handle on a daily basis. These are some of the same general weaknesses and reasons for the failure of every other committee which has studied and reported on education in the past. The usual conclusion of the reports of such committees is that teachers must be better trained and take more courses under the direction of the people and institutions represented by the people on these committees. Why we do not hear protests to these conclusions by regular classroom teachers and their union representatives is frustrating and disconcerting.

The substitute teacher, by the very nature of his work, has the true "insider's" view of a city school system. No parent, school board member, counselor, PTA officer or high-level school administrator can cover or work in as many schools in one year as most urban substitute teachers. Since a number of our substitute teachers work in a number of different school systems as they are needed, they have the "Insider's" view of a whole region of school districts. Where is there a State Department of Education administrator who can claim this wide experience? When new pro-

grams such as busing for integration, or enrichment programs are added to a city's system, it is the itinerant teacher
who knows where these programs are working, and where
and why they fail. When principals and other administrators
are too overburdened with administrative details, they may
not know precisely what is happening in the classrooms of
their own schools. However, the substitute teachers soon
find out when they have to pick up where the classroom
teachers leave off. Principals usually do not have tenure in
their positions, so they may not wish to speak out on the deficiencies of a school system for fear of losing their positions. Again, it is the substitute teacher who must manage
to deal with those deficiencies on a daily basis. Counselors
and support personnel usually see a limited number of students, and usually see them at the end of situations where
the student's presence in the classroom has become intolerable. Or they see students with very special needs. In any
case, these students form a small part of the spectrum of
student needs and behaviors. Since counselors usually see
students on an individual basis, they usually have a very full
schedule and cannot accept students who are giving a substitute teacher "a bad time." In a school district with budget
troubles these auxiliary personnel are few and far between.
In most urban schools the substitute must manage as well
as possible with the whole range of behavior and ability
with little or no expectation of help.

Here again, it is the substitute teacher who has the
widest range of experience upon which to make the most
sensible recommendations.

It is unfortunate that once again, the importance of
substitute teachers within the routine process of teaching is
being overlooked and ignored. All recommendations and

plans to improve education are ineffective unless all components including the substitute teacher are taken into account.

In the State of California, with its geographical boundaries stretching from Mexico to the Oregon border, and with these major coastal city areas attracting people from all over the world, it is small wonder that it is difficult to provide adequate public education for all students. In the Spring of 1987, the State Superintendent of Schools and the Governor of the State became involved in a highly publicized political argument over the issue of money and how much money was to go to public schools. The Governor, with the support of the Legislature, won, in that the Governor was supported in his decision to use surplus money for a small tax rebate for every California tax-payer. Many parents, and those who work in the public school system, considered that since this money did not go to schools, the children lost and their education suffered greatly. In our opinion, both the Governor and the Superintendent have been shortsighted.

In this incredibly diverse state, there are districts which differ more from each other than schools in different nations differ from each other in other parts of the world. Within districts, there are schools which differ as much as if they were in different states and different cities of this country. Since the late 1960's and early 1970's, many laws have been passed in an attempt to equalize these differences. Often, these laws have been written by people who have had little experience with children and no experience teaching in a variety of these schools and districts. Classroom teachers, by the nature of their assignments have worked very hard to stabilize situations in their own school and their own classroom. Some have had more success than others, depending on the students and the particular administration of their school.

Substitute teachers, on the other hand, have had the unenviable, but highly professional educational experience of teaching in many classrooms in many schools, in diverse districts, and in all grades in all these schools and districts.As an officer of SFSTO, UESF, and several times a member of the negotiating teams, Pam has addressed theSchool Board often on matters relating to substitute teachers, and she is aware of most of the issues which affect the entire school district and the entire state.

Preparatory teachers have taught all grades and therefore have had experiences which are partly those of the classroom teacher, and partly those of the substitute teacher. By drawing on their experiences as classroom teachers; I in a reasonably stable school in a middle-class area of Sacramento, and later as a music-preparatory teacher in a minority area school in Oakland, as well as a parent participating in PTA and member of the Substitute Teachers Organization; Pam as a substitute teacher and member of the Substitute Teachers Organization and with the United Educators of San Francisco; drawing together the experiences of other substitute teachers in San Francisco; I have come to certain conclusions and ideas for partial solutions to particular problems endemic to the public schools. If at times the tone seems angry, pointedly didactic, or lacking in gracious manners, I may agree to that criticism. However, those who have attempted to teach in some of the same circumstances as they, may feel that Margaret and Pam have understated the case. The main concern is that readers will take these criticisms seriously enough to raise questions with school boards, visit public schools, listen to the concerns of public school teachers, and write their conclusions to the Governor of California. If possible, send copies of the letters to the State Board of Education, and local school boards.

IV. What is it like to be involved in the grass-roots experience of requesting changes?

A Personal Report from Margaret Sigel

At 5:30 p.m., on the evening of October 27, 1988, a historic event took place in the street outside and later, in the board room of the Board of Education at 135 Van Ness Avenue in San Francisco, California. The San Francisco Substitute Teachers Organization staged a demonstration for more pay and better working conditions. Not only did substitute teachers walk in a line with placards, but certified, permanent teachers from the California Teachers Association and the American Federation of Teachers, joined in. So far as we know, this was the first time that such an event had taken place. For the first time, substitute teachers took their cause to the public. Pam Routh wrote the words; Marilee Hearn, Don Taylor, and Tim Murphy did the organizing; and I played the violin to keep the marchers chanting. As we walked up the stairs and into the auditorium to the "Battle Hymn of the Republic," school board members and the audience took note of our presence and union support. Unfortunately, and predictably, the newspapers which had been contacted did not send representatives and did not report the event, or describe our appeal. In the succeeding weeks of arbitration, the Board of Education did not acknowledge the reasons for our demonstration and continued to operate on a "business as usual" basis. But not for us substitute teachers. We have a functioning organization, and we expect that this essay will educate even more people who will support our demands for reasonable change.

The beginning of that change started when a student used foul language and swore at a substitute teacher. That teacher decided that he would not "take" insults as part of the usual difficulties of the teaching profession any longer. In 1981, Stephen Auerbach persuaded other substitute teachers to join him in forming the San Francisco Substitute Teachers Organization. As far as can be ascertained, it is the only independent substitute teachers organization to obtain a contract with a school district in California.

V. Why do school systems need substitute teachers?

Before describing the job of the substitute teacher, we need to understand one point very clearly: Education, to be effective, should not proceed by fits and starts. It is a long-term, continuous process. When a classroom teacher is absent, there must be a qualified person to replace him. When that qualified replacement, the substitute teacher, can pick up where the permanent teacher has left off, can maintain a sense of continuity, routine, and discipline, the students can continue to learn to master skills and understand principles of the subjects they are studying.

VI. What is the history of employment of substitute teachers and parafrofessionals?

A Brief History

In the "good old days," we were led to believe that

teachers were never absent from class. Since there was no such thing as sick leave, maternity leave, family illness leave, mental health leave, medical appointments leave, educational, or sabbatical leave, there was little call for substitute teachers. If teachers were ill, they waited for summer vacation to recover. If they were seriously ill, they left the system and another teacher was hired. Sabbatical leave was for college professors only.

With the growth of our large urban schools and districts, it became necessary to have a pool of substitute teachers to step in and help with the increased number of teachers absences. Still, those absences were expected to be very short, and the substitute teacher a very temporary replacement: in today's terms: a baby sitter, not an adoptive parent. This is unrealistic in light of today's needs for long-term substitutes. Many members of today's school boards still retain an image redolent of the thinking of the 1890's. They may be willing to put out money for computers, but are they unwilling to examine the financial needs for a reasonably paid group of itinerant, or substitute teachers? Moreover, they do not feel compelled to hire credentialed teachers for the job.

In the school year of September 1987 – June 1988, in San Francisco, there were usually not enough substitute teachers to fill all the classrooms when a permanent teacher was absent. During seven weeks of that year, substitute teachers filled more than 1,000 positions per week. The lowest number of classroom positions filled was 413 in June during the last week of school. When there were not enough substitute teachers to take the place of absent permanent teachers, the classes were split up among the remaining classrooms. Sometimes this meant that teachers took sections of grades which were different from the ones which they were teaching. In any case, class-size limits in school contracts were abrogated. In some schools, which regularly and chronically could not obtain substitute teachers, the demand for small class size was rarely honored.

Paraprofessionals

During the 1960's, school drop-out rates, learning failures, and discipline problems reached major proportions, particularly in so-called "ghetto" areas of urban districts. With the Head Start and Vista Programs, many otherwise unemployed people began to volunteer their time and energy to help teachers deal with classroom problems. Thus the paraprofessional movement came into being. Paraprofessional people have helped to solve many problems, but school test scores do not show that there has been that much improvement for the money expended. Some paraprofessional people have proved their worth, but there is not evidence that the system has improved vastly with their efforts.

In the last 30 years of flux and change in public education local school boards have consistently ignored the one personnel component which could have been the most helpful in solving the problems: the itinerant substitute teacher. Because of the way substitute teachers are used in schools, the possible positive aspects of their efforts, with their experience and talent, are usually lost, while the negative aspects are emphasized to the detriment of students, permanent teachers, individual school sites, not to mention the district, and the society which pays the bills.

VII. What is it like to be a substitute teacher?

The following section is an analysis of the difficulties inherent in a substitute teacher's position, and a description of some experiences in day-to-day substitute work.

Before a substitute teacher walks into a classroom he must apply to the school district which can check his qualifications. Many districts only require a Bachelor of Arts Degree. When a non-credentialed teacher is hired, he may only serve 20 days in the same classroom. When faced with a long-term absent teacher, many districts hire a succession of non-credentialed teachers. In San Francisco, the S.F. Substitute Teachers Organization worked to stop this practice. In many instances, substitute teachers have more experience, education, and knowledge than the teachers they replace. Substitute teachers who hold a credential have had training in long-term planning and have had at least ten weeks of supervised practice teaching. In their experience, they have learned to cover a broad range of subjects as they are used at various grade levels. What experienced substitute teachers offer that more permanent teachers may not have developed, is a flexibility to change quickly from one grade level of learning to another or from one subject to another. Planning ahead is more difficult for a substitute teacher than for a permanent teacher because a substitute does not always know how long the assignment will last: planning one day at a time requires different perspectives than planning for an integrated, long-range unit's study. Also, the experienced substitute teacher must often bring his materials to cover the blank spaces left by the permanent teacher, and those materials may not be left in the room at the conclusion of the temporary assignment. Although the problems may be different, the substitute teacher who has a California Teaching Credential, or an equivalent credential from another state, is a REAL TEACHER.

Now we must ask: What are the potential problems and possibilities inherent in the position of substitute teacher? The answers turn on a second question:

How well do the people involved know each other?

It can be surmised that the more information available to all parties, the better the working relationship. Familiarity is less likely to breed contempt than unfamiliarity. Within the context of change from one job assignment to another there are elements that can lead to difficulties and disadvantages to all persons involved. First, the substitute does not know the school, its personnel, or routine. Next, the temporary teacher is an unknown entity to the people with whom he works. Finally, there are subtle negative associations that are attributed to the substitute teacher simply because that teacher is not the person who is absent and therefore cannot fulfill certain roles expected or desired of the absent permanent teacher.

Let us first consider the strange and unknown elements confronted by the substitute teacher in each new class or school. He could well say, as Pam often says, "In every school, I do the same thing; in every school, it is done differently." Much teaching time is consumed in routine matters that are generally necessary, handled differently at each site, and for which one cannot prepare.

One example Pam gives is that in just such a simple matter as taking the school lunch count for a class, there may be an amazing number of options: Do children get their hands stamped in the cafeteria before school, so that the teaching personnel is not concerned with this procedure? How is it handled if the child comes in late? If the lunch count is taken in the classroom, who does it: the teacher, the paraprofessional, or a student monitor? Is money collected, or do students buy tickets? Is there a special envelope or paper that must be marked in any special way? Is it sent to the office with a student, or does a school monitor pick it up? If it is taken to the office by a student, how many normally may (or must) go, and how are they chosen? When is the count due? Is it sent to the office, or does it go directly to the cafeteria? What does the teacher do if he wants lunch also? Is he to put his money in the same envelope with the students? How much? How is he to pay if the money was due in the cafeteria before school?

Pam's analysis of a school day adds to this the many other routine matters that must be addressed during the day, including, but not limited to: How is roll taken? Who takes it, the teacher or paraprofessional? Is it sent to the office? When? How? Are children escorted to and from the classroom, yard, or cafeteria at recess, or lunch, or do they come and go on their own? What is classroom or school policy about children using lavatories during class time? How many children may or must go at one time? Is a nurse present on the school site? When? How should a sick child be dealt with? What if the phone system is not working? What problems does the neighborhood pose to children on the school grounds? Are gates locked or opened at certain times during the day? Who may come on the grounds, and who must not be on the grounds or reported to the office? Where does one find the answers to these questions?

What are the relationships with school personnel and students?

Relationships with Secretaries

The first person whom the substitute teacher generally encounters at a new site is the secretary. He is not only one of the first, but also one of the most important. In actual authority, the principal is the most important, but in effective authority, the secretary is the most important. By directing virtually all of the school's communication and traffic, the secretary controls much of what actually happens. The principal may set policy, but the secretary's actions may determine whether or not they truly work, especially if the principal is too busy or absent. At this point, the secretary may be too busy or harassed to supply the substitute teacher with the necessary answers to the above questions. The secretary's role as supplier of information and support for disciplinary matters is not necessarily voluntary. It may all be considered as an unwelcome and unnecessary burden, and other matters may have first priority.

At this point, the secretary may make a quick, prejudicial, unfavorable, and erroneous assessment of the reporting substitute teacher. With nothing else to rely on, such a judgment can be based on anything as flimsy as speech or appearance, or previous encounters with other substitute teachers. There is a vast area for error in assessment that may have to do with the personal skills, experiences, and prejudices of the assessor, and little, if anything to do with the new, temporary teacher who has come to do a necessary job.

As with every other group of people, secretaries "are human." Their attitudes can change from day to day depending on the stress and pressure under which they are working. Some go out of their way to help the substitute teacher get settled, others do as little as possible to help.

Often, the type of information and support reflects an attitude that the substitute teacher ought to know certain things automatically, and is a nincompoop if he doesn't, but on the other hand, he cannot be trusted to know anything. Obviously, a new teacher must request keys, his room number, directions, yard duty schedules, location of faculty room, and lavatories, changes in schedule, work room location, facilities for copiers. Also, teachers and other adults may be assigned to work with the class, and their schedules. This way, the substitute teacher can plan for surprise changes in the written lesson plan: on one hand, unexpected assemblies can be a relief; on the other, waiting for a special teacher or paraprofessional is not.

Permanent Teacher's Plans

It is in the contract in San Francisco that permanent teachers are to leave lesson plans to be followed by the substitute teacher. However, these plans can range from nonexistent (there actually isn't a teacher for that class yet, or the teacher didn't leave any). Other times they are not to be found, the materials to execute them are buried or non-existent. Some plans are so intricate that a great deal of time is spent looking for the components and trying to understand how to use them. Sometimes the plans are general enough so that a substitute teacher can follow them and add a few extra details of his own devising. Also variable is how closely the teacher or principal expects the plans to be followed. Either or both of these people may complain if the substitute does not add his "own thing" to the lesson. More often, there is a complaint if lessons are omitted, abbreviated, augmented, or changed. The problem is that in each new situation, the expectations change, and are rarely stated explicitly before hand. Lesson plans are usually in place for one day; teachers who know they will be absent ahead-of time sometimes leave them for longer, and that-is especially helpful and necessary if there are different schedules for each day of the week: for example, art class Tuesday morning, computer class Thursday afternoon, a library session Friday morning, and a special assembly on Monday. Sometimes, a special change in the whole school's schedule was announced previously, but had not been noted in the lesson plan, or it was posted near the permanent teacher's sign-in sheet, but not by the one for substitute teachers. At best, plans are provided for a week ahead. After that, most substitute teachers must rely on their own, using former plans as a guide. Unfortunately, the prevailing attitude among teachers who do return, is that the work done by the class under the supervision of the substitute teacher had nothing to do with the children's regular education. At best, he has "held the line." Pam Routh once taught a class for three weeks, having to invent a great deal of imaginative work. When the permanent teacher returned, she condescended to speak with Pam for five minutes, and then threw out every carefully graded paper (done on overtime) without even a glance at them. From speaking with other substitute teachers, this seems to be a fairly typical response. Some teachers want the lesson-plan routine followed to the letter, including minutely arranged systems of rewards, while others only ask that none of their equipment is missing. If lessons are produced with "wrong" information, material, or level of expectations, much criticism will come the way of the substitute teacher, even though no alternative plans had been provided for his use. Often the phone number of the permanent teacher is denied to the substitute even when requested in order to provide material for the class in the absence of the permanent teacher.

Relationships with Paraprofessionals

Pam has had extensive contact with paraprofessionals. Most of the time, they make the day vastly better than when there are none. However, paraprofessionals are a more complicated aspect of a substitute teacher's life. The issue of authority is more complex than with the permanent credentialed staff, secretaries, and principals. On the one hand, the overt authority is supposed to reside with the substitute teacher because he has the teaching credential and outranks the paraprofessional; most paraprofessionals do not have credentials. Sometimes a substitute is called just to meet the legal requirement to have a credentialed person in the classroom.

In truth, the paraprofessional may be the person who actually commands effective authority over the children for several reasons. First of all, the children know this person. For better or for worse, theirs is an established relationship. Occasionally, if the paraprofessional is weak or disagreeable, and hence, disliked, he may have minimal authority. Usually, however, the presence of a known assistant adds an emotionally stabilizing component to the children's environment. The children do not view this person just in the context of having past knowledge of classroom procedures and schedules, the locations of supplies, and of their needs and skills, but they recognize that he can also communicate their actions to "their" teacher at some future date. They are in some ways accountable to the permanent teachers through the paraprofessional in a way that is tenuous at best with the substitute. Accountability to the substitute teacher is established independently. Unless the children are convinced that the substitute and permanent teacher really do communicate, accountability is diminished. Children may also be aware that a paraprofessional has direct knowledge of or contact with their families, thus with the other source of authority in their lives.

As stated before, the paraprofessional usually knows the routine of the classroom, and the location of supplies. The substitute teacher, by contrast, will probably have to ask the paraprofessional about these matters. It is usually wiser to ask than not, but such deference to superior knowledge does not enhance the substitute teacher's image of power and authority, unless done skillfully.

Paraprofessionals, though lower in rank than other members of the permanent staff, nonetheless out-rank someone who is not a member of that staff at all. However, the substitute teacher has to be careful in allowing the paraprofessional to wield authority in matters of discipline. If done unwisely, the substitute teacher will be held accountable for the misrule of the paraprofessional. It requires a large degree of skill for the substitute to establish a reasonable working relationship with the paraprofessional in the brief and pressured moments they may have before the class of children arrive. If the paraprofessional is supportive, the class work will run smoothly enough for the substitute to be effective in his teaching; if not, the paraprofessional can undermine the substitute teacher's authority and the classroom atmosphere will deteriorate.

Relationships with Principals

A member of the non-academic public might easily assume that a principal would wish to meet the new substitute teacher, the strange substitute teacher who had come to work in his school and take charge of twenty-five to forty students for an unspecified number of days. Many substitute teachers also make that assumption until they are rudely awakened to reality. That reality is that most principals, for whatever reason, simply are not concerned about the body who takes over a classroom in the absence of a permanent teacher. The presently prevailing attitude of many principals seems to be that as long as the substitute teacher controls the discipline of the classroom so as not to send disruptive students to the office, that is (almost) all that matters. Pam Routh has had the following experiences with public school principals: "In the more than one hundred schools where I have taught, I made the acquaintance of fifty percent of the principals because I made it a point to introduce myself. In the other schools, some made it a point to speak to me, while others met me by chance. In some schools, when I chose to introduce myself, the principal rudely rebuffed me by saying that he had more important matters to attend to." Later on, there was no attempt made to arrange for a time to talk. Perhaps the principal was too busy at the moment, but the attitude of incivility then permeates other relationships with staff who also are "too busy" to answer questions important to the teaching of the class.

Pam also elaborates that in eighty to ninety percent of the schools she has visited, the principal has never set foot in the classroom during instructional time, even when I have been with the class for at least five days. When asked by the substitute teacher for an evaluation after ten days service, as per the negotiated contract, principals usually say nothing about classroom instruction, but rather concentrate on details such as clothing, appearance, voice level, classroom neatness, and whether or not the substitute teacher brought the children to the bus on time. Sending disruptive children to the office can earn a poor evaluation or a note to the teacher's folder saying that the principal does not want that substitute sent to his school again. How well or poorly the substitute teacher has worked with the children to help them learn their subject matter is rarely discussed for the simple reason that the principal has not been present long enough to find out. Rarely do principals take the time to ask the substitute teacher how the day went, or what the special problems may have been, or what should be noted for the future for the children or the permanent teacher. On the other hand, if the substitute is uninformed of school schedule changes, and happens therefore to meet his class five minutes late, he may expect to be roundly upbraided by the principal, and any other staff who may have been involved. Principals who at one time were, themselves, substitute teachers seem able to know the needs of the substitute teacher and give him necessary support and consideration.

There are a number of relatively simple solutions that can be used to ease the tasks of the substitute teacher. For instance, a few pages with a map of the school and immediate neighborhood with prominent landmarks and transportation points marked would be of immediate benefit. A list of staff, room numbers, schedules of special teachers, lunch counters and other procedures, and special events would answer most of the questions which the itinerant teacher must ask.

Relationships with Peers: The Teaching Staff

The attitude of the permanent teachers toward substitute teachers is far less positive than it should be. Permanent teachers view substitute teachers as temporary, not to be taken seriously, and as less than competent. Their prejudice does not recognize substitute teachers as "real" teachers. They only tolerate them as an unfortunate necessity. Fortunately, this prejudice is not common among permanent teachers who at one time were substitutes. The following story illustrates these attitudes: A teacher offered a substitute teacher a ride. Another permanent teacher asked, "Why are you giving him a ride? I don't even talk to substitute teachers!" These attitudes show up in cooperative teaching situations where supervision or instruction is shared. When a substitute teacher enters a new school, his peers know nothing about him and there is usually little time to explore background, competence, knowledge, or willingness and ability to cooperate. It is small wonder that the permanent staff members have little hesitation in correcting or countermanding directions given by the substitute teacher and doing so in front of the children, thereby undermining all the authority of the substitute teacher. In most schools, all teachers are on the same work schedule, so it is difficult for permanent staff to assess the work of the substitute teacher. Even so, there is an enormous amount of tattle-tale gossip which goes the rounds: stories of substitutes who put their feet up on the desk and read the newspaper, as well as those who imposed their own plans on a class instead of following the lesson plans. Inadvertently, there are all sorts of minor, but irritating social gaffs which a substitute teacher may commit: sitting in the favorite chair of a permanent teacher at lunch may engender criticisms which have nothing to do with the substitute teacher's ability to work with children in the classroom. The worst problem for the substitute is, as Pam labels it, "not being the person who is absent." For example, if the teacher next door wanted to borrow a book from the absent teacher, he may feel disappointed and thwarted if the substitute does not have or cannot locate it.

What is even worse; sometimes, the unwitting substitute becomes the "scapegoat," or the pawn in long-standing faculty rivalries and animosities. He is sacrificed because he is temporary and has no one to take his side. It is convenient to blame or accuse the substitute for the failures of others, again because there is no one to take his side and he will soon leave the scene of the dispute. When a substitute teacher attempts to behave in a professional manner by attempting to maintain the continuity of the class and informing the permanent teacher of progress or difficulties with various students, his efforts are rarely acknowledged upon return by the permanent teacher. Information is rarely exchanged and less effective teaching is the result.

As long as their teaching peers think of and treat them as inconsequential subordinates, to be dealt with out of sheer necessity, the full potential of substitute teachers cannot be realized. This negative attitude is reinforced by the principals, and the administrative staff of the school district.

It is also reflected in the level of salaries and the way they are regulated. A day-to-day substitute teacher has one of the most difficult teaching situations that exists. In spite of the need for people who will do this work, they are paid at the lowest rate on the scale no matter that they may have more background and resources to offer than the permanent teacher. If substitute teachers were paid at a daily rate that took into account their years of experience as well as their academic credits, and was equal to the permanent teachers' rates, there probably would be enough teachers available to fill all classrooms where the permanent teachers are absent. Of course, budgets would have to be revised, as "differential pay" would no longer go to teachers who have used up their sick leave. The "differential pay" situation pits permanent teachers against substitute teachers and certainly makes for a "conflict of interest" for unions who try to represent both groups. The recognized unions who represent teachers have given so little consideration to substitutes that they were not even aware that a conflict of interest might have existed.

Relationship with Students

The most obvious group of individuals affected by the substitute teacher's presence are the children. Here, there is a collective as well as individual response for the substitute teacher to manage. In the vast majority of cases, the substitute teacher will have to deal with more students than principals, secretaries, counselors, paraprofessionals, custodians, and parents combined. Although other people may have more authority to ultimately affect the career of the substitute teacher, it is the reaction of the students that is considered to be the formal objective of the teacher. As we have seen, the factor of "change" has been built into the substitute teacher's expectations. He has taken it for a given, or chosen it for an option, and therefore has developed some specific strategies to deal with it.

The children, however, may experience having a stranger thrust on them as an unpleasant or even threatening surprise. "Their" own teacher started out as an unknown; a person who might be suspected or tested. Often, however, if the children have passed kindergarten or have siblings who have been in the school previously, there is some reputation to precede the teacher. He is an object of injury, speculation, and rumor before he is actually the children's teacher. Such information may also pertain, though to a lesser extent, to a substitute teacher who has worked extensively with other classes in that school at a previous time. The "new" teacher and the beginning teacher have a common struggle to establish their authority. However, the permanent teacher has the weight of the authority of other staff members, especially past and future teachers, to support him.

An effective permanent teacher has probably established a well-understood routine that encompasses classroom rules and disciplines, the schedule of subjects studied, and the assignment of extra duties. Obviously, some routines are better than others. However, any routine is better than none at all. Usually, the permanent teacher and the students have fought their battles over this routine as well as the class rules and their enforcement. The substitute teacher is ignorant of these overt, particular rules as well as some of the unspoken conventions. The children view the "new" teacher's ignorance as disconcerting, disquieting, or even as an outright threat. Since children seem to learn better when they know what to expect, the substitute teacher must "catch on" and reinforce the pre-existing routine as quickly as possible. Change for children is certainly not welcomed with eagerness; new procedures and directions are viewed with suspicion. The substitute teacher's lack of knowledge of their basic routine undermines his authority. Although they have fought with "their" teacher over the old routine, having to accept a new one from a stranger is rarely considered a positive prospect. Only a surprisingly interesting alternative may gain a fair hearing from the class. The children develop a loyalty to the permanent teacher in the face of an implied attack on his authority, and the implied incorrectness of his rules and procedures by the introduction of new expectations from a stranger.

A substitute teacher must walk a psychological tightrope between finding out "normal" procedures and following them as closely as possible, and determining strategies that work better for his own personality and style. Then he must introduce them in such a way as to gain a high rate of acceptance. Usually, the slower that the changes are made, the better.

Children, however, must also be trained to accept changes from adult authorities, and to recognize the right and necessity for substitute teachers to do things differently. The substitute teacher is not the only person who has different rules and a different personality from "their" teacher. Even at the elementary level, children are confronted with other staff teachers, librarians, resource teachers, music, art, and dance specialist teachers, guest lecturers, and community workers such as police and firefighters. There needs to be a standard of courteous conduct extended to all adults along with a working realization that each of these people may require a somewhat different response than those with whom they have previously worked. Small children may be expected to feel more threatened by change than older ones; yet it can be said that they have actually experienced a faster rate of change than older children who have settled into experiences of longer duration. A measure of a child's maturity may be his ability to accept reasonable change.

Part of the resistance to the substitute teacher's changes may also be part of the syndrome of his "not being the person who was expected." If the children expect certain promised rewards for accomplishments or good behavior, or expect special events, and the substitute teacher cannot deliver on these expectations, the disappointment may become a negative assessment of the substitute teacher, and a negative element in the students' behavior. The substitute, quite simply, represents the cause of the disappointment. For example, if the substitute teacher can't do a special art project since the supplies are at home with the absent teacher, the substitute teacher may then be "blamed" for denying them the fun, even though it should be obvious that the substitute had no inkling that such a lesson had been previously planned before he had accepted the job that morning. The emotion of "blame" is not a rational sentiment in this case, but as subtle or subconscious as it may be, it still taints the children's acceptance of the substitute teacher. This directly affects their behavior.

Some of the attributes unique to the substitute teacher may indeed be explored and accepted by the children, as they were with "their" teacher, but any short-comings may be exaggerated by the temporary nature of the contact. Suspicion of the motives and attitudes of the "new" teacher may be emphasized by the children's knowledge that this person might not intend to stay. As with "their" teacher, the longer and more persistently a substitute teacher insists on enforcing his way in a routine matter, the more loyalty he accrues. Where there has been a turnover of substitute teachers for a class, it becomes more and more difficult for each subsequent teacher to establish control and authority. Even where the reasons for turnover may have had nothing to do with the students themselves, the students begin to perceive that they can control who leaves or stays. In a class where the original teacher left because of student misconduct, the students try to test out each newcomer. A substitute teacher who opts to stay with such a class has to establish that he has no intention of leaving, and that routines and standards will be enforced. This is "easier said than done." In fact, it is probably impossible unless the teacher has administrative support and "back-up" for discipline meted out for all infractions of rules.

Obviously, the more a permanent teacher prepares a class for the possibility of having a substitute teacher, the greater the possibility of the substitute teacher's success. Preparation may range from general instructions to the children as to how they are to treat a guest teacher, to what extra projects the guest teacher may use, at his discretion. If a teacher knows he will be absent, he may assign more detailed projects and information. It is at this point that effective follow-through by the substitute teacher will enhance his effectiveness and the quality of his teaching. Finally, the substitute teacher is quite aware that any complaint made by a student is given more attention by administration, staff, or parents than any evidence of work done by the class.

Relationship with Parents of Students

When a substitute teacher comes to take charge of a class, it is unlikely that there will be any time for him to learn anything of the family background of the children, including who is the parent or guardian and whether or not there are any siblings in the school. Usually, no relationship has been established with any of the people who influence the children's attitudes, performance, or behavior. Compounded with the substitute teacher's lack of information and the lack of time to get it before taking on the class, is the parent or guardian's lack of information. Usually, they do not know that there is a substitute teacher unless the child informs them of the fact. Many children do tell their parents, but the child may have any number of reasons for not doing so, one of which may be a fear of a report about his poor conduct in class. Most of the time, substitute teachers on short term assignments have neither the time nor energy to contact parents with notes or phone calls unless there has been a major problem, and even then, many substitute teachers think it futile to contact parents if the assignment at that school is finished. If the substitute teacher is assigned to a class for more than a couple of days, it is worth the time to contact the parents about any outstanding behavior or performance, whether it is good or poor. Rarely does the principal inform the parents that there is a substitute teacher in the classroom, even if that teacher has been there for a week or more.

Substitute teachers who are teaching a class during the parent-teacher-conference period of the school year have the same difficulties as permanent teachers in trying to persuade parents to come at a scheduled time. When parents fail to leave a current working telephone number on file, or children fail to take home and deliver notes, communication is non-existent. The greatest problems for substitute teachers are the complaints of children to their parents. It is not unnatural for children to complain, but often they are misunderstood, exaggerate, or unfairly harmful to the career of the substitute teacher. Children who have been reprimanded for poor conduct or nonperformance of their studies may be expected to have the greatest number of complaints. Unfortunately, since the parents don't know the substitute teacher, this may lead to their complaining to the principal that the teacher was physically abusive. Disciplining children by any means in the classroom has its dangers: the majority of children who go home and accuse substitute teachers of abuse are usually the students who have been the least cooperative and most disruptive in the classroom. It is not unknown for children to deliberately make false statements in an attempt to make trouble for the substitute teacher. Some parents are indifferent to their children in the first place; therefore it is not surprising that their children often have problems of conduct. Other parents set the example of combativeness by being prepared to declare that their "angel" can do no wrong, or at least not the wrong that was ascribed to him. This indifference leads to the lack of any enforcement of reasonable behavioral standards at home that might be transferred to use at school. The defensive-offensive parent denies the necessity of such measures, or is in direct conflict with their implementation: "How dare you make my son sit on the bench for ten minutes at recess: the other boy started the fight! I'll have your job for this!"

If the parent has kept contact with the permanent teacher, there is some stable, common ground for communication and discussion of expectations. The parent and teacher know each other, at least superficially. With the substitute teacher, the parents are totally ignorant of his personality, teaching, and disciplinary techniques, training, experience, and attitudes. There is a vast psychological space for wariness, defensiveness, cynicism, underestimation, and suspicion of the teacher on the part of the parent. The only information to support confidence in this stranger is that the district saw fit to hire him. Under these circumstances, if there is discussion and conflict, the parents are more likely to take the word of their child against that of the substitute teacher. Fortunately, there are some honest and realistic parents who know their children well enough to recognize and admit it when their children break rules and stretch or bend the truth.

However, in many instances, substitute teachers who walk into a new setting are extremely vulnerable. There is probably no one on the staff of the school who knows the substitute teacher and his record or performance well enough to introduce him to the parent or back him up in a dispute. The parent is a more permanent part of the scene and his reactions must be dealt with for a longer period of time. The substitute teacher is temporary, and if too much "trouble" with the parents is generated by his actions, even if those actions are totally legitimate and necessary for the education of the class, the principal may well avoid having that substitute teacher come back, let alone discuss the complicated and unfair consequence of the outright accusation of abuse reported by the child.

Basically, the substitute teacher is in a very vulnerable position. The longer he works with the class, and the more he contacts the parents for positive reports and consultation, the more positive and effective the relation with parents and students will be, and the closer it reflects the position of the permanent teacher.

VIII. What are some remedies?

The logical theory is that the better a substitute teacher is known, and the more he knows about a school, the more effective he would be. It might be best if the substitute teacher in a large urban district would work for, by mutual consent, a limited number of schools (with flexibility to meet district needs). The more familiar he would be with the schools and the more they would be with him, the less factors of "being unknown" and "unknowing" would get in the way of positive teaching. Under these circumstances, adjustments to circumstances by the substitute teacher and "the school" could be made mutually. Practically only the initial contact would be confusing. As the person came into more contact with each school, he would become an increasingly "known" and "regular" part of the staff, solving many of the problems described.

The fact that simple solutions have not even been considered for these problems is a clear indication of the totally muddled thinking that marks most of the operations and relationships of public education in general. So long as simple problems with simple answers are ignored, large problems requiring careful thinking will continue to remain disaster areas.

Therefore, we are directing this discussion to you, the substitute teacher, in the hope that together we can start to make a change for the better.

IX. Why is making change for the better so difficult?

When we suggest change, everyone will tell us, the substitute teachers, that the system is in a period of crisis and that we should wait until that particular crisis is past before making changes. Our memories go back as far as 1941, to the California school crisis of World War II. This was a time of large population shifts, due to the need for and the huge influx of war workers from other parts of the country. Since that time, Pam and I cannot remember a single year that did not have a "crisis" situation in education. If substitute teachers continue to wait for a period of relief from a crisis situation, we may well still be waiting by the middle of the 21st Century. The argument to wait until a crisis is past is therefore indefensible.

Change implies that more money be spent on schools. Administrators will tell substitute teachers that there simply is no more money available. Anyone who has observed the recent fight between the Governor and the State Superintendent of Public Instruction knows that the money is in the State treasury, but the Legislature and the Governor do not wish to spend it on public education. This too, is a very old story: if the schools succeed in doing a good job of teaching, the government says that more money is not needed; if the schools do a poor job, the government says the schools don't deserve it. Either way, we lose. What no one wishes to admit is that substitute teachers have been subsidizing public schools all of their working lives by taking money out of their substandard wages to buy books, resource materials, extra paper, pens, pencils, crayons, and many, many other necessary supplies. While legislators have increased their own salaries, substitute teachers have gone without increases. The argument that there is not enough money in the treasury is also indefensible.

The Governor has formed yet another "Blue Ribbon" committee to study school fiscal needs. This committee of people with long past government experience and even longer titles will not be expected to solve any problems. Its main task is to buy time for the Governor. Nothing will be changed in the tax situation or in the allocation of public monies. The public schools will not be helped, and the Governor will have an alibi for not considering the needs of substitute or permanent teachers and students. Just as with the previous arguments, this argument, that substitute teachers wait for the "Blue Ribbon" committee's conclusions, is indefensible.

X. Why must public schools and their substitute teachers be supported?

There are good and sufficient reasons why we must have public schools, and also why substitute teachers must have the necessary authority to teach and enforce behavior standards in the classroom. However, for those who do not understand the need for public schools or the need to give sufficient, effective authority to the substitute teacher, let me state some ideas and conclusions which may be drawn from our history experience.

"Independence," as in the "Declaration of Independence," is a word enshrined in our national consciousness as well as a goal for our individual lives. The men who wrote and signed the Declaration, and who later framed our Constitution, were educated men. They considered their ability to read and write as a necessary part of their intellectual equipment which enabled them to direct their own lives, to try and live in harmony with other human beings, and to serve as leaders of a new country.

What would these men think if they were alive today and observed our society as a whole as well as classes in progress in particular in our public school system? Let us indulge for a moment in this time-warp fantasy. As these honored men strolled around our cities, it would be obvious to them that no citizen, female or male, black or white, foreigner or native born, could function as an independent person without the ability to read and write and to decode the multiplicity of signs and directions that meet our eyes at every turn. They would certainly see the public schools as a necessity even though they, themselves, may have been educated by tutors or in private academies. They would surely wonder how we could expect our numerous and varied citizens to work together and manage to continue to uphold the principles of the Constitution which they had so laboriously constructed, if we lacked public education.

Yet, when they would observe some classes in progress in our public schools, they would surely wonder if we had taken leave of our senses. What would they think of the lawless students who so often manage to disrupt the studies of the majority of the class? What would they think of the system which refuses to give authority to the substitute teacher who wishes to teach law-abiding students? It is possible that they would consider that the Constitution and our system of government might be in real jeopardy. They might also consider that the dangers to our government stem largely from forces of ignorance within our borders, rather than from forces outside our borders. Therefore, we propose that we make a few important changes in our thinking about educational policy and classroom management of California. Cities and states may then take note of our success and follow our example.

XI. What New Attitudes Must Be Adopted?

First, we must rethink our own attitudes towards ourselves and our wish to work off our aggression toward authority and those who would curb our anarchical impulses. There are places and occasions where this may be acceptable. However, those places and occasions are not in the classroom during the time for teaching and learning, or on the school playground where students should be socializing, playing, and exercising with friends. Classroom lawlessness is not funny or excusable. It is also not affordable for the tax-paying community. Parents who disagree with this should be invited to take their children out of the public school system and be required to pay for private education or teach their children at home following a state mandated curriculum.

Next, we must rethink the idea that substitute teachers must psychologically manage and control lawless students if they wish to be considered as good, employable substitute teachers. Most substitute teachers are quite able to deal with lawless students on a one-to-one basis outside the classroom setting after the school period or school day is over. They do not wish to take class time to discipline one or more students in front of a whole class. Few adults enjoy, or wish to air their personal transgressions and mistakes in public; why should students in trouble not be given the courtesy of some privacy in working out their problems with the adult in charge?

Substitute teachers are hired to teach a full class for a prescribed period of time. They are not hired as "custom-tailored" psychological therapists to give a troubled child total therapy and attention at the expense of the whole class. If parents insist that the substitute teacher give this kind of attention to every disruptive, troubled child, then they must be willing to pay the rate which therapists charge. At the going rate of $50 per hour per child, there are substitute teachers who would be delighted to take the job. However, at the going rate for many substitute teachers, i.e., 50 cents per hour per child, this kind of request is totally unacceptable. Parents who continue to hold that opinion must find a school system which will pay private therapy prices for every child who may at some time be unhappy or disruptive.

A third point which we must rethink is the idea that substitute teachers who dismiss disruptive students are poor educators. This is simply not true, but this idea is sometimes promoted in order to continue to take advantage of substitute teachers financially as discussed in the previous paragraph. Good substitute teachers dislike using threats, bribes, corporal punishment, extra homework assignments, sarcasm, seat-changes, detention, withdrawal of privileges, verbal abuse, or calling parents in order to enforce discipline so that the majority of the students may learn. When a substitute teacher has the authority to dismiss disruptive students, none of these time-consuming, unprofessional strategies need be used. The flow of the lesson can be maintained, and the substitute teacher is free to help students with learning problems. If parents wish to denounce substitute teachers who dismiss disruptive students, then they, themselves, should be willing to take the time to sit in class and help keep potential and actual trouble-making students from disrupting class work.

A fourth and last point which must be reconsidered is the idea that the principal has more important things to do than to deal with disruptive, troubled students. What could be more important to the running and the purpose of the school than sorting out these problems? If there are many disruptive students in a school, then it is the job of the principal to enlist the help of cooperative parents in finding ways of supervising those students when they are dismissed by the substitute teacher. There must exist responsible, reliable adults who are consistently available to supervise. The principal is paid a higher salary than any substitute teacher for the very reason that the tax-paying public expects the principal to assume the difficulties that go with the resolution of these problems. Principals may have many other responsibilities placed on their shoulders, but the tax-paying public considers all these other responsibilities to be secondary to the primary one of helping all teachers maintain a reasonable classroom atmosphere for learning. When principals are given to understand that this is their primary task, and that they may not coerce substitute teachers into keeping disruptive students in class through the use or threat of unsatisfactory evaluations and failure to rehire, they may begin to take constructive measures. At present, for the first time in San Francisco school history, since there are not sufficient numbers of substitute teachers looking for work, principals who have used these tactics in the past are finding that the "word" has gone around and substitute teachers won't come to their schools. Parents have started to put pressure on the principals, and have taken their problems to the administration and school board. Now principals could organize themselves, and force a recognition of the problems within a district. Parents who don't wish to help principals and support their demands for help in supervising disruptive students may be invited to form their own schools and meet the problems themselves, under state supervision.

XII. A New Perspective

A Personal Reminiscence from Margaret Sigel

Toward the end of World War II, in the town of Wells, Nevada, the principal of Wells High School was searching for a qualified mathematics teacher to teach in the high school. All of the young men who had taught mathematics in the past had been drafted. So far, none had returned from service. The Principal persuaded my friend, Ula Mae Vandiver, a qualified, retired mathematics teacher to return as a substitute teacher until the end of the term. She had retired some years earlier, not only because she could afford to do so, but also because she did not wish to deal with students who were disciplinary problems.

When she took over this class, Mrs. Vandiver found one student who refused to follow her directions. He persisted in teasing other students by pointing the sharp end of his geometry compass in their faces. Mrs. Vandiver immediately reported this to the principal, and stated that she would leave rather than put up with this disruptive, dangerous behavior. The principal knew that he could not bully my friend into changing her mind, and he also knew that he could not find another qualified mathematics teacher. He asked Mrs. Vandiver why she had not reported disruptive behavior in the past. "I didn't think you would back me up" was her answer. To his credit, he told her the truth, "You were right." He took care of all the disciplinary problems until the end of the War. At least for that short period, the needs of students and their education were served. After the War, education and the rest of the Country returned to "business as usual."

As you will see from the contents of the following letter, it was still "business as usual" with the public education system nearly forty years later. After 1984, I tried in every reasonable, possible way to "go through channels" to bring about change. No one wants to deal with the problem of school discipline, or the substitute teachers' need to dismiss disruptive students without prejudice to their careers. We hope that the following discussion will persuade school administrators, teachers, and the general public to try to understand this problem and give teachers necessary support.

Margaret Sigel
San Francisco, California

May 1984

An Open Letter

The Hon. William Honig, Superintendent of Public Instruction, State of California Sacramento, Calif.

Dear Superintendent Honig:

On January 3 of this year, I started a job as a music specialist teacher for a Bay Area elementary school. Two and a half months later, I resigned. The following will explain the reasons for my resignation. I hope that my experience and conclusions will point up needed reforms which could only be carried out with the aid and direction of your office.

I was not given authority equal to my responsibility. I was not provided with the means to exercise authority in a judicious, effective, swift and visible manner, and this is the cause of the discipline problems which I experienced in my classroom. When these problems mounted to an intolerable degree, I resigned.

I am an experienced teacher and I never had had any problem teaching music in the classroom. In recent months, I was a docent for the San Francisco Symphony Orchestra. I went to six elementary schools in my area, and I had a most enthusiastic response to sessions of music appreciation to prepare the classes for trips to Davies Hall to hear the Symphony perform. Between four and seven classes and their classroom teachers attended each of these sessions. There were no discipline problems.

My background in music and teaching was more than adequate to meet the responsibilities of the music specialist job. The district was hiring specialist teachers at this time as part of a strike settlement agreement. I was to take each class for a fifty minute period once a week, thus freeing the classroom teacher for fifty minutes for preparation of material for the class for the rest of the week.

During the Christmas vacation, I went to the school to meet my new principal and see the facilities. Ms. W. impressed me as a most able, competent professional of the highest standards. The faculty, as I became acquainted with them, impressed me in the same manner. They did everything in their power to give me help and support.

Then why did lack of real authority lead to a discipline problem so great that I had to resign? None of the easy stereotypes about the make-up of the student body explained the difficulty. In the end, I decided there were three major factors to the problem. Those factors were accepted tradition, the California Education Code, and the limited budget of the school district. All this was summed up for me when Ms. W. told me that each teacher was expected to take care of discipline problems within the classroom. They did not have the space or the supervisory personnel to deal with any except the most severe discipline problems. Then one would have to work through channels and the Code, and that would take time.

This is virtually the same thing I heard over 25 years ago when I started teaching first grade in another district in California. This is the same system which was in effect when I was an elementary school student in different districts in Southern California. At that time, the public school system was under great stress and criticism. During and after World War II, many war industries workers came from other parts of the U.S. and their children had difficulties adjusting to new schools and new situations. The regular classroom teachers had great difficulties enforcing discipline, but the music teachers had the brunt of the problem. The discipline code was not then and is not now equal to the discipline problem.

Ironically, it was a very good class experience which clearly showed me that the lack of effective authority was indeed the root of my discipline problem. In one particular first grade class, I had concluded that most of the students were too immature or that my simple plans were too advanced for them. Only coloring their own pictures seemed a suitable activity for them. Then, more than two months after I had started teaching this class, Ms. M., their classroom teacher brought them to me and said, "You will have a good day as Those Four Boys (her emphasis) are absent."

She had finally succeeded in suspending the class clown and three would-be guerrilla rebel leaders for the afternoon. They would not be vying with me for the leadership of the class. The remaining twenty-three students came in calmly and quickly took seats since they did not have to avoid the miserable behavior of the now missing four. I then was able to proceed with a lesson which included telling the story of Peer Gynt, listening twice to Grieg's music for the story, drawing charming and recognizable pictures for the story, and finally, singing several "old favorites" and learning a new song. The children's obvious delight, pleasure, and self-control was in such marked contrast to previous sessions with this class, that I could scarcely believe it was happening as it was happening. When Ms. M. returned and observed this, her pleasure was so great that she did not know whether to laugh or cry.

The lesson I have described was the one I had planned to teach the second or third week of my assignment. It had taken two and a half months for the lucky and unpredicted day to arrive. Those four boys were back on the school ground the next day and were quite unrepentant. After all, it was the classroom teacher and the vice principal who had exercised authority.

Those boys would be ready for me with their old tricks next week. If I wanted to suspend them from my class, I would have to "go through channels" with phone calls to parents, parent conferences, and conferences with my principal or vice-principal. As I had 21 different classes and four to six such students in each class who needed this type of attention, I wondered where I was to get the time and energy to deal with the legitimate needs and interests of the other 475 students.

I wonder how long law-abiding students and law-abiding teachers are to be kept from learning and teaching by the miserable, disruptive behavior of a very few students? I know that parents feel that a student cannot possibly learn his school subjects if he is dismissed from class. What must be understood is that a misbehaving student has only one intention — to learn more successful tricks of misbehavior to disrupt the class. It is the rest of the class who are kept from learning. My experience leads me to wonder what would happen to the test scores for the majority of students in the regular classroom if teachers could quickly and effectively dismiss misbehaving students from the class. Would those misbehaving students pull their tricks as often if they were quickly and effectively deprived of their audience of the rest of the class? After teachers have had years of preparation, study, and teacher training, should they then have to take courses in "aggressive discipline" in order to teach the three R's — not to mention music, art, science, history, geography, not to use drugs and firearms, fire safety, health habits, nutrition, first aid, and how to safely cross a street? Why not let those teachers who are interested in discipline and social behavior supervise those students who need it, and allow the classroom teachers to teach subject matter to the students who are ready and wish to learn? I would particularly expect that substitute teachers as a group would find their work easier if they could quickly dismiss trouble-makers. The rest of the class would not then suffer if the regular classroom teacher had to be absent.

As I was signing my resignation papers, the Personnel Director said that she did not expect a reform of this kind in her lifetime. You, as Superintendent of Public Instruction for the State of California were elected to office with many reform promises in your platform. You have succeeded in restoring a great amount of money to the school budget. Now, I challenge you to see that all teachers have proper and effective authority so as to properly and effectively teach the majority of students who are in their care and wish to learn.

This is an Open Letter to invite other teachers and those interested in education to comment on my remarks and to send their ideas to you.

Yours truly,

(Mrs. John) Margaret Sigel

XIII. What are the reasons for disruptive students?

By now, we must ask why there may be disruptive students in a well-run classroom in the first place. Why are there students who don't want to learn?

First, we ought to remember that learning is a demanding exercise of the mind and body. Not all children come into a classroom with their minds and personalities ready and willing to submit to the discipline of the classroom and the substitute teacher. The substitute teacher is just one person with a very limited supply of books, pencils, paper, and a few other assorted educational materials. The substitute teacher is NOT a television studio production team who can pull out new and astonishingly interesting sound and sight sensational experiences every fifteen or twenty seconds of a five hour day. A substitute teacher can interest and motivate, but the process is not easy or simple, and it is only the bare beginning of education. After the substitute teacher has developed some interest, she or he must direct, help, prod, support, explain, review, and constantly repeat material until most of the students can finally understand and incorporate skills and insights into their daily life. No television set or computer — for all their touted ability — can truly do this job as well as a good substitute teacher or permanent teacher. But then, a substitute teacher cannot ever work to the best of his or her ability if one or a group of students decides to usurp classroom authority because they are unwilling to follow classroom discipline. Very often mechanical aids are used as a way of simply bribing or entertaining students into reasonable behavior. These aids are often extraordinarily expensive, but the school district purchases them in the hope that they will "solve" the discipline problem for the principal.

Also, many children come into a classroom from a home environment that operates without structure, planning, supervision, consistency, language development, responsible authority, consideration of others, or loving care and kindness. It is not possible for a substitute teacher, particularly a day-to-day substitute teacher, to remake the child into a nicely behaving student in the first thirty seconds of greeting at the beginning of a lesson period, so that the child can accept direction along with twenty-nine other students from diverse cultural backgrounds. If such a child becomes aggressive toward the substitute teacher or other students, the safest and kindest strategy which the substitute teacher can use for all concerned is to dismiss the child to a supervised area of the school where he/she can sit until he/she has calmed down and is ready to submit to the reasonable discipline of the classroom. The substitute teacher should make the determination as to when to try and see if the child's attitude has changed. If the substitute teacher wishes to wait until the end of the period in order to work on a one-to-one basis with the student, that decision should be respected by the principal. A few schools in some districts have made these arrangements, but they are few and far between.

XIV. Why are there limitations on the dismissal of students from class?

We must remember that children, even more than adults, are social animals. Dismissal from a class is more alarming to them than any other form of punishment, just as refusal to talk to a child in a family group is a very alarming form of punishment in that environment. Dismissal from class is also the most effective manner of helping the child to calm down and rethink his/her demands for attention from others. If an aggressively acting-out child can be dismissed to a supervised area for in-house suspension until the end of a period, the substitute teacher can then talk to him/her on a one-to-one basis where he/she has no chance to enlist the support of twenty-nine other children. The child can then be brought back to the classroom on a trial basis as a socially responsible member. Small reminders, rather than open conflict should bring about cooperation from the child. The authority of the substitute teacher may then be accepted.

Now we may ask why substitute teachers have customarily been given so little authority to dismiss students from class.

Originally, most substitute teachers were women and most principals were men. There was then a definite disinclination to give real, rather than pseudo-authority to women. That time is long gone and should be so recognized. A new law has been enacted by the Legislature. Any substitute or regular teacher may now use Public Law #813 as the basis for support in a decision to dismiss a disruptive student from class. One reason for a lack of support for the provisions of #813 is the attitude of some parents. There are parents who have memories of substitute teachers whom they disliked intensely, and in their discussion of those memories they inadvertently "egg" their children on to act out their own long past anger and aggression. This cannot be tolerated by substitute teachers. Under the new law, it does not have to be tolerated.

There are some parents who will claim that racial discrimination is the basis for dismissal. In most cases, this is simply a cover-up by the parent to excuse the fact that his/her child has not been trained at home to respect reasonable authority. If the parent truly feels that discrimination is the root of the trouble, he/she has the right to go to the school, sit in the classroom, observe his/her child's behavior and that of the substitute teacher. The law does not support racial discrimination and the substitute teachers know this. They do not support racial intolerance either. Principals may say that they do not have the time to deal with disruptive students. We have already discussed part of this problem. However, we must remember that principals have often found time to deal with these problems if the teacher was a regular teacher well thought of by parents. Principals use the "no time" excuse as an alibi to substitute teachers since they know that substitutes will not be in the school long enough to generate a power base with parents. Under the new law, there is no sound reason for a substitute teacher to tolerate this kind of lying, sub-standard, unprofessional behavior on the part of any principal.

Parents may say that a child is not learning anything if he/she is dismissed from class. On the contrary, the child is learning one of the most important facts of life, which is: his/her ACTIONS HAVE CONSEQUENCES. Now let us examine this part of the educational process in greater detail.

XV. What is the "Learning Experience"

Several years ago, some students broke into Lowell High School when the school was not in session. Their object was to rob the money from the potato chip vending machine. In trying to do so, they set off the silent alarm to the police who came immediately. When the students were confronted by the police, all but one ran away. This one student pulled out a toy gun which was a reasonable facsimile of a real gun, and he aimed it at the police officer. The officer saw it as a real gun, drew his own revolver, and shot the boy dead — instantly.

In the ensuing investigations and reports over what the policeman might have done or not done, over the grief of the family, and the background and character of the student, one point was not mentioned, the obvious one: that no one had managed to teach this student that actions bring consequences. In his sixteen years or more of life, this student never understood that he could pay with his life for an unlawful act.

Now we know that all unlawful acts do not necessarily bring instant death as in this case, and that all lawbreakers are not immediately apprehended. Still, that does not excuse substitute teachers from teaching that "Actions bring Consequences." It does not excuse substitute teachers from enforcing reasonable discipline in our classrooms. We are not doing our students any favors by allowing them to usurp the authority of the substitute teacher who then cannot teach and demonstrate that "Unlawful Actions bring Consequences." The most effective and most humane means which we have at our disposal to teach this concept to troubled students is to dismiss them from class; since State Law #813 gives substitute teachers the right to do so; since it is clearly in the best interests of the class to do so; and since, in the long run, it is clearly in the best interest of the troubled, disruptive student to learn that "Unlawful Acts are followed by Consequences," substitute teachers should not feel constrained to keep these misbehaving students in class on the possibility that we will receive a poor evaluation from a misunderstanding or incompetent principal.

XVI. How can substitute teachers help to make changes?

Now we come to the most difficult part of the problem: how are substitute teachers, the lowest ranking members on the educational ladder, going to bring about change?

The first step, in case it has not been done in your district, is to bring together substitute teachers and form an organization. Some of your potential members may already belong to the American Federation of Teachers, and others may belong to the California Teachers' Association, so the substitute teachers, may ask why there should be a separate Substitute Teachers' Organization. Ask yourselves, what have either the local AFT or the CTA done for substitute teachers lately? Have they helped you, the substitute teachers, get pay raises, benefits, recognition, help with discipline problems, money for supplies, better working conditions, legal counsel in grievance procedures, or a reasonable contract? Have they ever suggested that they would stand behind you the substitute teacher, in case of a strike, or bargain for you so that you didn't need to consider a strike? If the answer is "no," then ask them why not. The number of CTA and AFT locals who have organized substitute teachers and included them in their membership are relatively few and tend to be concentrated in large urban districts. Even when they are included, substitute teachers are viewed as another faction competing for limited resources. The needs of substitute teachers, who are usually a minority segment whose membership is constantly changing, are often the last and least addressed. The problems and concerns of permament staff often seem preeminently important to the other union members. The experience of San Francisco substitute teachers, when they became members of the larger permanent teacher union (which is both AFT and CTA) is that the union is constantly finding problems which seem critical and more important than any substitute teacher needs. If local organizations further say that they would like to help substitute teachers, but that they are terribly busy studying all sorts of problems, you will understand why we advise you to form your own group. You could wait until the middle of the twenty-first century before substitute teacher needs take a priority in teacher union groups..

Even if your substitute teacher group cannot get recognition from the local district school board, you should organize. It will give you a base for moral support, raise your morale, help you distribute information, raise your self-esteem, give you a chance to meet the other terrific people in your profession, give you an organization to speak for you in the local newspaper and help you to contact other substitute teachers organizations. Most importantly, it will give you a group to collect funds with which you can hire a lawyer and pay a bargaining agent. Once the organization is in place, the organization can apply to various charitable foundations who are interested in improving education in the public school system. Alone, you are at the immediate mercy of the principal and the district administration; as a member of a group, you have added strength and counsel in times of distress and difficulty.

Once your substitute teacher group is organized, try to bring together information: What is the teaching-time per month or year that substitute teachers cover classrooms in the district? How many years are teachers given for leave so that the district hires a substitute teacher at a lower salary rather than drawing from the list and granting probationary status? Does your district have the practice of transferring a day-to-day substitute teacher on the day before long-term status would be granted to finish out the time that the regular teacher is on leave? Who are the principals who give help with discipline problems? Who are the principals who give low evaluations to substitute teachers who dismiss unruly students? How do your salaries compare with substitute teachers' rates in other districts? Do you get unemployment benefits in the summer? What kind of medical insurance do other substitute teachers get? Few, if any of these questions will be answered by one substitute teacher working alone. Together, there is a true possibility that you can get this information, and then begin to take action in light of what you learn.

Information by itself is just a starting point: Incorporated into a lively, interesting weekly column written for a local newspaper, this information changes public opinion. If it is incorporated into a cleverly drawn cartoon or comic strip, the public may comment on it and start asking questions of the members of the community portrayed in the pictures. Interviews with members, and profiles of substitute teacher organization officers will generate interest and appreciation of the skills and abilities of substitute teachers and the organization. If a newspaper is not immediately interested, write up a one-page flyer for distribution with a PTA bulletin, or a neighborhood organization newsletter. This kind of publicity activity may not bring immediate results, but it does generate a climate of opinion which is very hard to ignore when "push comes to shove" in Board of Education meetings, grievance proceedings, and negotiations.

When looking for ways to change public opinion, we need not always "dance to the music" which others provide. Indeed, it is time for substitute teachers to stop being "suckers" for all other good social "causes." By the nature of our career and commitment to education, we are on lists of names and are asked to donate money to many worthy causes, "save the environment" funds and all the artistic and socially supportive organizations ask for our money and support. Not last on the list are our own Alma Maters from whom we earn our degrees and teaching credentials.

True, it isn't easy for these causes and institutions to raise money for their work but they do have sufficient funds to hire people to do the job: witness the fancy brochure, photographs, and post-paid return envelope. Committees of wealthy people sit on their boards and bask in the glow of success and newspaper coverage for their parties and fundraising events which substitute teachers cannot usually afford to attend no matter how much one might wish to support the "cause." These are often the very same people who fail to support the public school funds when "push comes to shove" with the Governor and the State Legislature or the local school board at contract negotiating time. These are also the people who are off to Paris and London and couldn't possibly be bothered to speak up for substitute teachers. Therefore, it seems time to wake up these people with a letter rather than a check. If every substitute and permanent teacher would buy one package of paper and use the ditto machine to turn out copies of a letter explaining why there was no check in the envelope, the volume might very well arouse some worthy cause board member to realize that the meetings he should be attending are those of the local school board. Here is a sample letter. It should inspire others to write their own.

Pam Routh

San Francisco, California

Prior to Summer 1989

Dear Sponsors of a Very Worthy Cause:

I have received your literature requesting a contribution and have reviewed it carefully. I hope you will give my letter the same thoughtful attention and consideration, for the benefit of us both.

Your cause is extremely well worth supporting,

and I wish I could help. Unfortunately, I must put this letter, instead of a check, in the envelope you sent me. It embarrasses me to say I cannot afford to help you, but this is why:

I am a substitute teacher for the San Francisco Unified School District, and I have been attempting to earn my living from them since 1974. From then until now, substitute teachers have been the economic scapegoats of the District. As the least powerful and most temporary employee group in the District, substitute teachers have received the least and last support.

We currently receive $80-$85/day, which is only 60-65% of a beginning teacher's pay of $134/day. In 1974, we received $44/day, or 87% of a beginning teacher's pay. In those fifteen years, permanent teachers have received well-deserved yearly raises that have nearly paralleled the 160% rise in the cost of living, while substitute teachers went the seven years from 1974 to 1981 without a single penny wage increase and only a 93% increase in wages in the fifteen years.

Many substitute teachers have more experience than the teachers we replace. Long-term substitutes and teachers on the tenure-track receive pay increases for experience and extra education; day-to-day substitute teachers do not. Neither do we receive any sick-leave, or medical or dental benefits, as permanent teachers do. If we are injured on the job, workers' compensation gives us only a small part of our wages, but we receive no compensation if we acquire one of the highly communicable diseases we're exposed to (more frequently than permanent teachers).

Salary comparisons with classified personnel and even some levels of paraprofessionals show that we are one of the lowest paid categories of workers in the District, especially when one considers the benefits obtained by (almost all) the other groups. Considering that permanent teachers are not compensated adequately, substitute teachers, who comprise 10%-25% of any school day's work force, are truly underpaid. Gross earnings for the school year (180 days) are $14,400-$15,300. That is if I receive work every day; I am not paid for any day in which there is no work, and my service depends on the whim of the District. During the ten-month school year, there are several unpaid holidays, which reduce the gross monthly (twenty-day average) income of $1600-$1700. As a Children's Center teacher, I may be able to work summers and some holidays, but assignments are usually less than the standard seven hours, which means I earn less.

I live in a city that has been described as having the fourth highest cost of living in the world. The apartment in which I lived until recently, was "only" $550/month. Rent control kept the price from going much higher only because I have lived here for ten years. Even with rent control, that expense has risen 50% in the decade. On this scale, a substitute's wages are at poverty level.

I am a fully credentialed elementary school teacher; I had to attend college for five years to get my certificate. Many school districts, including San Francisco, are experiencing a shortage of qualified substitute teachers. Instead of raising the wages (some still pay less than $50/day), many districts are lowering standards. Even though San Francisco presently has only credentialed teachers, several other districts permit people with no formal training to enter the classroom. (It's difficult enough to do a competent job with training.) This means that the policies of some local school boards are harmful not only to substitute teachers, but to permanent teachers, administrators, the general public, parents, and most importantly, to the school children. To sacrifice quality for the sake of economy is destructive.

Other occupations and industries offer wages that are in drastic competition to those of a substitute teacher and require less education and training. (The custodial staff of the District earns more than substitute teachers. The pay for cleaning toilets is greater than the salary for teaching the District's children.) In the last two decades, women have had increasingly extensive choices of occupations; now that there are more options, teachers and potential teachers are taking them.

If there has been progress made in San Francisco, it is because a very disgruntled group of substitute teachers formed (in 1981) the San Francisco Substitute Teachers Organization and obtained a small raise as a start. In 1985, after two-and-a-half years of bargaining, the S.F.S.T.O. obtained the only contract that we know of between a school district and an independent substitute teachers' bargaining agent. We have been back at the bargaining table for the last two years, trying to bring in the second contract. Meanwhile, permanent teachers obtained a raise last year, are also back at the bargaining table, and will undoubtedly receive an annual raise. Because I believe I should work actively and effectively for what I believe is equitable, I am a member of the S.F.S.T.O. bargaining team.

I believe that substitute teachers will receive equitable treatment only when the State of California sets a (high) minimum wage for substitute teachers, as it does for beginning permanent teachers. Teaching is the only profession in which temporary personnel does not receive at least a per diem (the minimum daily rate for that occupation). In the meanwhile, public monitoring of local school boards could help. We need all the assistance we can get. The inequitable treatment we receive affects the children of the society and prevents many substitute teachers from making financial contributions to worthy causes. Everyone is affected; perhaps you can help us, so that we can help you. In the meanwhile, your envelopes must remain empty.

Sincerely,

Pamela A. Routh

Change Through Government

Do not expect that a change of the membership of any Board of Education will change the procedures of the district or the way you will be treated as a substitute teacher. Some elected officials and many appointed ones have only two concerns: getting re-elected or reappointed and trying to stay somewhere within the budget, which, in education, is always totally inadequate to do the job. Other officials feel too harassed and pessimistic to make the necessary effort.

You have to understand that only a few, if any, government officials in any capacity want to muster the necessary political support to help solve educational problems. Without a permanent educational crisis about which to complain, many officials would not have any issues to discuss with the public at election time.

Once elected, government representatives disappear behind a wall of aides, meetings with ghost committees, and a smoke-screen of ceremonial appearances. All responsibility for the actual educational process has been so divided up that no one can be held responsible for anything of any substance or have a relationship to what actually happens in the classroom. The substitute teacher, being the adult in charge of the classroom is therefore charged with total responsibility, and, of course, the least pay. We also are the target of the public anger because everyone else who should be taking the criticism has ducked out and run away. In spite of all this, a substitute teacher may be able to survive, but it will probably have more to do with luck than design and more to do with one's ability to stand up for one's rights, or "take it on the chin" rather than one's concern for children or expertise in teaching them.

To meet these problems both permanent and substitute teachers have insisted on unions, negotiations, bargaining procedures and strikes because they have seen that the use of sweet reason rarely produces progress, either for teachers or for students. Teachers know that the public school system is not a production line, but they have come to realize that board of education members are usually subject to the political pressures of the business world, whether that pressure comes from large corporations in a sprawling urban environment or the owners of small shops on the one main street of a small rural community. Labor contract negotiation vocabulary seems to be the only language understood by administrators and members of local school boards.

XVII. Why don't present negotiations work?

Negotiations and Logic

During negotiations, school board members and others have stated, "Negotiations have nothing to do with logic." This pronouncement has been made (to Pam) in negotiating sessions with the certainty, knowledge, and pride of someone who imagines he is delivering the Tablets of the Law from Mount Zion. Fortunately for those who are not content to act in accordance with this motto, it is very easy to see that it need not necessarily be accepted. It has been repeated parrot-like without any indignation or critical thinking on the part of the representative of the school board and the District negotiating team who cannot begin to recognize the consequence of this point of view. From Pam's and my own experiences with negotiators, the process often seems frustratingly irrational: after one has presented all the logical reasons why one's own proposals are logical, just, fair, possible, and for the benefit of all concerned, one faces rejection and counter proposals that seem illogical, unjust, unfair, unworkable, and for the benefit of the very few.

Just because the process has worked out to be illogical doesn't mean that it always must be or should be so. The process of labor negotiations (bound by law in this country) is less than one hundred years old. It most assuredly has gone through changes in rules and procedures over the years. The people engaging in it have surely become sophisticated in the give and take of informal and formal processes. None of these processes has been written on stone by the Diety. Some have been written into the law, but none of them is in the Constitution or its Amendments, and all law is subject to formal change.

We contend that bargaining should be subject to logic, and the lack of it perpetuates inequity, injustice, and the defeat of educational progress. In the long run, it is the students who suffer from an improperly negotiated teachers' contract settlement. The people who tell us "The bargaining process is not logical," should say that with the greatest sense of shame and remorse, and with every intention to work for a change.

In previous generations of students living in the 18th and 19th centuries, the apprentice system, the guilds, and the use of child labor on farms, in mines and factories siphoned off the majority of students before they finished eighth grade. This has not been so for some years, but school budget finance is often predicated on this part of history. Business people are finally beginning to realize that all life is much too complicated and fast-changing for any business to use illiterate employees (this is true for farmers as well). Neither can our society afford to support a mass of illiterate, unemployable young people. Also, some business people are beginning to understand that the cost of re-educating illiterate employees is higher than they can afford: the public school system is the only tax-supported system which can come to their aid. Unfortunately, their understanding of the educational process is so limited that they constantly support expensive, glamorous sounding programs while refusing to support the known and necessary, but long-term programs. They are always looking for the "quick-fix" which doesn't exist in education, no matter how many people pursue that will-o'-the-wisp ideal. The upper echelons of the educational hierarchy have been only too happy to tell business people all kinds of things in return for support. However, it is usually a substitute teacher who has nothing to lose who could tell the unvarnished truth, and is therefore the true "expert" who should be consulted about educational problems. Unfortunately, in the past many substitute teachers feared they would not be rehired if they "blew the whistle" on district policies and therefore they did not speak out and contribute their knowledge.

XVIII. Change Through Choice and Preparation

We should remember the expression: "To be forewarned is to be forearmed." This is particularly true when looking for a teaching job, but we cannot expect that any university schools of education will help substantially in this process. Their job is to keep their own jobs by supplying a steady flow of new teachers. They may continue to add courses to their curriculum, and to add more requirements for more degrees and specialized fields. It is not their job to change the conditions under which substitute teachers must teach and control classrooms. They have also totally avoided public criticism of graduates who have entered school administration. When have they seen fit to bring back graduates for discussion of conditions encountered in public school work, or provided a forum for discussion or for change?

By asking the right questions and circulating the answers; by taking the time to observe classes and investigate resource centers, substitute teachers may be able to discriminate between districts and set up a rating system as to which districts are helpful to substitute teachers and which are disaster areas.

One essential question to ask of any district administration is, "What are your grievance procedures?" A district without such procedures for substitute teachers is a potential disaster area. Look for a job somewhere else. However, if enough people would ask that question before signing any contract or substitute list, a district which needed substitute teachers, might just become sensitive to making that first step toward change by instituting a grievance committee and reasonable grievance procedures.

XIX. Managing to Survive in a "Worst Case" Situation.

To some readers, this section may seem rather didactic in style. However, our purpose is to be direct and emphatic enough to penetrate the mental torpor which one often experiences while reading some of the more arcane educational treatises purporting to teach teachers how to teach. Only a very few such texts discuss the realities of how to handle classroom discipline in "worst-case" school districts. This is our attempt to help substitute teachers find a new direction which does not repeat all the mistakes of the past.

If you have been assigned to a "worst-case" class in a worst-case school, you must first develop a mental attitude that will help you survive. Until this point in your life, you may have been a conscientious person who always did a job to the best of your ability and tried to stay on the job until difficulties were worked out and the job completed. Unless you are built like a football linebacker and/or have found some other way to be physically intimidating without lifting a finger, you will find that these exemplary attitudes of yours will work for your self-destruction.

Instead, take the attitude that you will only stay on the job long enough to earn what you need to survive until you can find a job where the boss will give you the support and authority you need to do the job for which you were hired. The world of education has never been structured in a reasonable manner on these issues and no one has any intention of changing it for your convenience or success. If you complain, you will only have to listen to a litany of horror stories which demonstrate the staying-power of the person to whom you have complained. Again, this is a profession which seemingly has no intention of solving its problems or taking account of the justified criticism which is mounting against it.

As a substitute teacher, you must also change your attitude toward the society and community who have hired you. You must understand that although government officials and most spokespersons and parents say they are in favor of education, in reality, they have acutely ambiguous feelings about education which they may not wish to examine in public. Many communities actually fear that you will succeed as a teacher. This is the only logical explanation for the fact that a number of school districts are, in fact, warehouses for the containment of young bodies until such time as they can be absorbed into the labor force doing repetitive work. This is probably why the term "local control" has been elevated to a kind of sacred status by most boards of education including the State Board of Education of California. Witness what has happened in the Oakland School District in 1995, with another strike worse than 1983. There are also many politicians who would be very upset if you succeeded in teaching students to read and reason. These politicians prefer to have a functionally illiterate constituency whom they can control by harangue and cliché speeches. If you have difficulty in controlling your class, as indeed you may, you must not condemn yourself or see yourself as a failure. Neither should you consider that your principal, or other school administrators were necessarily successful in classroom control when they were teaching in these same circumstances. If they had been truly successful as teachers, they probably would have stayed in the classroom instead of running for an office job in which they shuffle papers. If they had had the expertise to handle classroom control and enjoyed teaching, they ought to have stayed in the job of teaching, and ought to have used that expertise to push for higher wages for all teachers. With an office manual and a few weeks of study, you could probably do their administrative job as well or better than they do. They cannot do your job as a substitute teacher well, and they proved it by leaving the classroom.

You must also recognize certain things about yourself: You are not a saint who can hope or expect to solve all problems. Recognize that the school has problems and that the administration has failed to solve them. It is not your fault if you cannot solve problems in a day when those problems were a number of years in the making. You should not talk yourself into being the "fall guy" for these problems. Do not allow yourself to be "brainwashed" into believing that if you, the substitute teacher, were just a little more caring, or better organized, or more intelligent, or had that "special" ingredient, you could be successful. Yes, it is true that there are people who are successful in the field of substitute teaching. The most important quality which they have is the ability to analyze what they need to succeed and then demand it, or find the place where they can get it. They move around and make plenty of mistakes until they find the right combination. Of course, all this will be hidden from you, the beginning substitute teacher, unless you have the opportunity to dig deeply into their past and sort out the special circumstances which made that success possible. You have to decide if you have the physical stamina and enormous sense of humor necessary to accept the difficulties and are willing to follow their example.

A scenario for possible survival in a "worst-case" situation.

If the preceding discussion has not sent you, the substitute teacher, looking for a job in some other field, and you have no choice but to accept a job in a "worst-case" school and district, here are some ideas to consider and use.

1. Be sure you have a key to your classroom. Always lock all doors and close windows before leaving the room. Do not allow anyone to stay in the room when you are not there. Do not have any students stay in the room during recess, and do not have students "help" you in the classroom before or after school or during the noon hour. Child abuse, and sexual abuse accusations may be lodged against you and you would have no defense.

2. On the play-ground before class, look over your group as they start to gather when the bell rings to start school. Notice the ones who are continuing to fight or who seem unwilling and unable to control themselves in the line. Go over to them, and, in a low voice, ask them their name. If they are insolent and refuse to settle down or give you their proper names, tear off sheet #1 and say to the child, "I have a note for you to take to the office right now!" At this point, one or two children may copy the first child. Send the most disruptive to the of-

fice. You now have the possibility of having a line or group of children whom you can instruct on the proper way to behave and walk to the building door without killing each other in the process. If some start fighting in line, don't hesitate to send more to the office with note #1, which reads: "Please detain this child under your supervision until I request to have him/her sent back to the class. He/she is participating in a 'learning experience.' The substance of that experience is that 'Actions bring Consequences.' This child's actions were: fighting after the bell rang, (or) pushing in line, (or) continuing to talk, yell loudly and disturb others after being spoken to by the substitute teacher after the bell rang."

3. When you, the substitute teacher, are still on the playground, (or in the hallway if it is raining), stop your line and compliment those children who are standing quietly and listening. Then, say, "As you noticed, several children have been sent to the office for a 'learning experience.' They are learning to take responsibility for all the parts of their bodies. Their actions have brought consequences. You have learned to keep your hands and feet to yourself and to keep your mouths quiet."

4. At this point, the children who have been sent to the office may be coming back down the hall. Be sure that your classroom door is still locked. Do not open it. Say, "Only those students who have learned our first lesson will be allowed into class and will be counted present." Ask one of the students in line to tell the other returning students what they must do and remember about themselves. If they are still insolent and appear to be uncooperative, send them back to the office with "learning experience" sheets #1 and #2, which reads: "This

child needs more time in your office to study and understand sheet #1. Please read it with him/her and detain him/her until I send for him."

5. Most of the class will now understand that you truly "mean what you say," and you can now see if the line leaders can quietly enter, put their lunches away, and take their seats. They must remain quiet while the rest of the class follows their example. Do not tolerate any misbehavior. If eye contact and a simple gesture or reminder to be quiet do not bring immediate results, send the disorderly child to the office. Up to this point, you have established the fact that you will not tolerate disruption, that you do not hesitate to dismiss disruptive students, and you do not have to raise your voice to bring compliance with your standards for behavior.

6. Now the difficult part begins. The principal or the counselor may have read the notes and may have realized how many students you have sent to the office. You, however, now have most of the class under control. When the principal knocks on your door, you sweetly invite him in and thank him for bringing the remaining students. Do not allow those students to take their seats. Ask some members of the class to tell the principal their name and what they have just learned about taking responsibility for themselves, their actions, and all parts of their bodies. Then state that they have also learned to raise their hands and wait to be called on before speaking. Always ask the student to address the principal. Then ask each of the formerly misbehaving students to tell the principal what they have learned. If they refuse, you can say, "It appears that this child has not learned that 'Actions bring Consequences.' He/she

needs to think this over until the end of the period when I will come to the office and talk to him/her on a one-to-one basis. It is my professional practice not to keep disruptive students in my class. If you wish to understand my educational philosophy and discipline standards, you are free to borrow this book, Dear Substitute Teacher for the day." (Hand him a copy which you keep with you for just such situations.) "Thank you for coming to our room. I trust I shall not have to send any more students for a 'learning experience,' but if there are others who cannot take responsibility for themselves, I will not hesitate to send them to you."

7. At this point, most principals will be happy to say "thank you" and take the difficult student to the office for the rest of the period.

8. If, at this point, the principal decides to give you a "learning experience" by giving you a "dressing down" in front of the class, you are prepared: you pick up your coat, and any other belongings. Hand him the register and say, "This is now your job!" Leave! (Working as a maid in a motel or in a gas station is better than killing yourself in this job.)

9. It is just possible that the principal will walk out after you and ask you to stay. It is also possible that he will threaten to "black-list" you. In that case, say that you will be happy to go through a grievance procedure over this. This is not pleasant, but it is just as much trouble for him as it is for you. If this is his way of dealing with all substitute teachers who send disruptive students to his office, his whole attitude has become thoroughly counter-productive to his job as principal and it will

soon become obvious and painful to his superiors.

10. At no time should you raise your voice, use nasty words, or start to cry. Just be very brief, definite and matter-of-fact in every way. If he does not want to take over your class, tell him that you will stay if he makes it clear to the class that he will hold your disruptive students in "in-house-suspension" until the lunch period. Then you will both discuss discipline matters.

11. The rest of your morning should be reasonably livable. Be sure to collect all papers from your students. You can now use them for your own "Catch 22." If the papers are poor, then you should point out how difficult it is for any of the students to learn anything when there is constant disruption within the class on a daily basis. You have not taught them on a long-term basis so you can hardly be held responsible for this poor work. If the papers are well done, point out how much better these students function when there is quiet in the class and you can give help to all students. Since these students are obviously law-abiding, you see no point in sacrificing their best interests while dealing with the disruptive few. If the principal still insists on a poor evaluation, request the right to send a letter to the parents of the students in the class, stating what has happened.

When you discuss discipline with your principal, remember to emphasize that your actions were your educational procedure to provide a basic learning experience for the student. Knowing that his actions will produce consequences may at some time save this child's life. Furthermore, you do not consider that it is professional to subject a whole class to verbal abuse or correction just because a few lawless students insist on disrupting class activities. You are not going to bribe a class into good behavior. You are not going to force the other members of the class, in the name of "peer pressure," to assume what is actually adult responsibility for enforcing proper behavior of these few students. You are not hired to save the "face" of the principal. You have not been hired to solve the problems of the school district, the school, or the principal. You assumed that, as an experienced principal, he would expect to deal with students who have serious behavioral problems. Also, you assumed that he knew that some of these students had behavioral problems, that others had had difficulty in dealing with these particular students, and that you could not be expected to succeed where others obviously had failed. If others had succeeded in working with these students, they would not now be disruptive just because their regular teacher is absent. You also assumed that the principal would respect your adult manners and experience and the decisions you had made in the light of that experience. If, at the end of this discussion, the principal still insists that you may not dismiss these students, you may cite State Law #813. This does give you the right to dismiss. However, the principal still retains the right to refuse to hire you again and may place a poor evaluation in your record. You will probably have to take this up with a grievance committee. Here are some ideas you may wish to remember:

Most competent principals will back you up, take the disruptive students out of your class, and will not consider you a poor substitute teacher for dismissing those students. Most incompetent principals will balk at dealing with your disruptive students and will downgrade you on your evaluation.

Most principals have gotten where they are by "paying their dues." That is, they tried, and at least for awhile, they were able to survive without dismissing disruptive students. They may have been good teachers, but in similar miserable circumstances, they probably did precious little teaching. They may have survived by using the commonplace strategy of sending notes home and calling the parents on the phone and complaining about the student's classroom behavior. In many cases, they may have done this with the almost certain knowledge that the parent would beat and physically and verbally abuse the child into submission.

Teachers and administrators who use this strategy know full well that when children are beaten because of the complaint, those children will respect the teacher's authority. Those same children will usually also have extreme difficulty in learning any subject which requires reasoning ability. Beyond first and second grade reading, writing, and numbers, children treated in this way are generally too angry, resentful, frightened, and stressed to learn to use reason in figuring out mathematical "word problems" and to learn grammar and sentence structure to be able to write paragraphs on the subjects of their studies. For all practical purposes, the education of those children has stopped before the end of the third grade.

At some point in their careers, many principals have done what I have advised you to do. That is, they have left that particular school and that district and have gone looking for a district where students come from reasonably stable homes and, for the most part, have reasonably stable personalities. There they have advanced their careers and have been very careful not to "rock the boat." Principals who have stayed in "difficult" districts have their own troubles and will therefore probably not look kindly on your attempt to teach and survive by rocking their boat.

As has been stated before: working with disruptive students; taking them out of the classroom so that substitute teachers can teach the majority of students; finding ways to educate and help these difficult students should be the main responsibility and first priority of principals. However, the majority of principals will probably flatly reject that idea. On your totally inadequate substitute teacher pay, they expect that you will maintain a "saintly" personality and manage these students. It simply is not possible to do that and teach the rest of the class at the same time. It is "Catch 22." Principals expect you to do this because they have failed to analyze the discipline problem, and they have refused to look for solutions which will truly help and allow substitute teachers to work to the best of their ability.

Many principals have professional standards, but they have not been able to take the following steps before now. However, the substitute teacher is not responsible for the fact that exhaustion or lack of support from the community may have been the reason these steps were not taken. Principals must hold themselves accountable for:

1. Organizing themselves as a group to state and uphold professional standards, and to make those standards public.

2. Analyzing the discipline difficulties which all teachers face every day in their classrooms.

3. Attempting to analyze and state the best ways in which a principal can and should be willing to help teachers in dealing with disruptive students.

4. Analyzing why their time is so taken up with secondary,

peripheral issues having insufficient, or no time to deal effectively with disruptive students when a classroom teacher or substitute teacher so requests.

5. Stating remedies such as eliminating some of their "paperwork," or getting more help — voluntary, or paid — to do it.

6. Organizing workshops and conferences with community leaders to demonstrate to them what the budgetary needs are for supervising and educating disruptive students.

7. Using and supporting the PTA to lobby the legislature and the Governor to get the necessary monetary help long before the budget is submitted to those bodies for passage.

8. Hiring their own lobbyists to carry their message to every legislator.

Principals have failed to do this effectively and they expect substitute teachers to pay the price. Recognize that the price is too high and that you should not attempt to pay it.

This sorry, unprofessional state of affairs may very well continue indefinitely. The Governor continues to take a strong, but fluctuating stance on financing for schools so that at present, local control and reasonable planning are almost impossible. The public schools have their back "to the wall," and a few of the more intelligent administrators know it. Under these straightened circumstances, they will not be able to "deliver the goods," and many among them will then be out in the cold looking for jobs — even as substitute teachers. There were several such members in our own San Francisco Substitute Teachers' Organization, so this is not an example of wishful thinking on our part. Prin-

cipals and school administrators can be just as blind to political reality as any other group of people. They may complain bitterly over the Governor's refusal to give schools
available money, but they refuse to recognize that he was
elected by a majority of the voters in the state of California.
School administrators also refuse to recognize that in order
to be elected, the Governor has had to muster support from
many diverse groups who were willing to back his campaign
with large amounts of money. The Governor could not
maintain his stringent budgetary stance if he didn't know
that he had support for doing so. What that support is saying very clearly is that many school administrators have
been doing a terrible job over a long period of time. The
Public is asking: If the principals don't help classroom
teachers and substitute teachers to help students, who
needs principals? If school district administrators don't
help principals to help teachers, who needs to pay district
administrators? If the State Superintendent of Education
and the State Board of Education can't help district administrators to help principals to help teachers to teach students, who needs the State Superintendent and the State
Board of Education?

Only you, the substitute teacher, "has what it takes" to
force a change for the better in the public school system. I
hope this essay will be of some help in clarifying your thinking and pointing a direction for action. Pass it on to your
friends.

Sincerely,

Margaret Sigel